REAL CASTLES

digital time traveller

Mike Corbishley & Michael Cooper
Illustrated by Dai Owen

TAG

ENGLISH HERITAGE

TAG Publishing Ltd
25 Pelham Road, Gravesend, Kent DA11 OHU

First published by TAG Publishing Ltd 2000
in association with English Heritage
10 9 8 7 6 5 4 3 2 1

A CIP catalogue record for this book
is available from the British Library

ISBN 1 9028 0401 5

Reprographics by Scanhouse UK Ltd
Printed in Hong Kong/China by Wing King Tong

The Real Castles team:

Text	Mike Corbishley, English Heritage
CD design & programming	Michael Cooper, emcee multimedia
Narrator	Jilly Bond
Book design	Alan McPherson
Technical co-ordinator	Tom Baird, TAG Developments Ltd
Creative director	Tony Wheeler, TAG Developments Ltd
Cartoon illustrations	Dai Owen
Other illustrations	Terry Ball, Paul Birkbeck, Philip Corke, Peter Dunn, P Edwards, Ivan Lapper and Alan Sorrell
Photography	all English Heritage Photo Library or English Heritage Photo Library / Skyscan Balloon Photography except for British Library 20&38; CADW 26tr; Mike Corbishley 20tm, 34bm&35bl; Dover Museum 35tr&37bl; Michael Holford 28; Imperial War Museum 35tm&br

Contents

TA-RAAA!

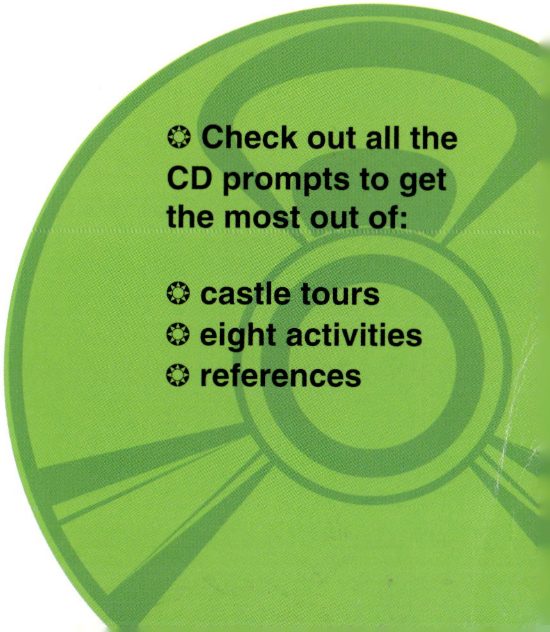

Check out all the CD prompts to get the most out of:
castle tours
eight activities
references

About Real Castles

Real Castles is part of the *Digital Time Traveller* series of interactive, history resources. The book, CD and web site have been designed to work together and provide everything you need to get started. The CD-ROM contains lots of useful things to help you to explore the development of castles.

Ace activities

There are eight on-screen activities, including your own Morse code kit. Of course, there are loads more things to make and do in this book – for example, why not play a game of fox and geese with a friend? (See page 20.) Time to get busy!

Top tours

Sit back and enjoy your own tour of Dover castle. The tours have been specially-recorded and include panoramic scenes for you to explore.

Crazy clip art

On the CD, you'll find lots of free clip art. How about making your own medieval-style greeting cards? With a little imagination, there's no limit to how you can use the pictures. (See page 42.)

References

Examine the evidence for yourself! The CD-ROM includes additional information to help explain life in a castle.

Wicked websites

For those of you with access to the Internet, there is a selection of brilliant web sites to visit for more information about castles – all at the click of a button! (See page 44.)

System requirements

Check you have the right sort of computer to use the CD-ROM.

Windows users

If you have a Windows PC you will need:

- a multimedia PC
- Windows '95 or higher
- CD-ROM drive
- super VGA monitor or better
- sound card with speakers or headphones
- 8MB available memory (RAM) (16MB recommended)

A printer, modem and Internet account will be useful for some of the on-screen activities.

Note: this is not a networkable product

Apple Macintosh users

If you have an Apple Macintosh you will need:

- 040 processor or better
- System 7.1 or above
- 640 x 480 monitor set to 256 or more colours
- CD-ROM drive
- speakers (usually built-in) or headphones
- 8MB available memory (RAM)

A printer, modem and Internet account will be useful for some of the on-screen activities.

Note: this is not a networkable product

Getting started

Follow these instructions to load and run the *Real Castles* CD-ROM.

You only need to install the CD once, but put the CD in your CD-drive each time you play

- Put the CD into your CD-drive (label-side up)
- Double click on My Computer, and then on your CD icon which will be called 'Castles'
- Double click on the icon 'setup.exe'
- Follow the on-screen instructions

Starting *Real Castles*

- Click on 'Start' in the task bar
- In Programs go to 'Castles CD'
- Double-click on 'Real Castles Start'

If your computer does not have Quicktime™ installed, click on QuickTimeInstaller.exe.

You do not need to install Real Castles. It runs directly from the CD-drive.

- Put the *Real Castles* CD into your CD-drive (with the label pointing up)
- Open the CD from the desktop
- Double-click on the 'Real Castles' icon

Using the CD-ROM

Finding your way around the CD-ROM is easy. Just click on the menu buttons and you will discover the main sections:

Guided tours

Click here to visit the three castle sites. You can choose to take a guided tour or explore each of the sites independently.

Click on the green arrow buttons to go to each site

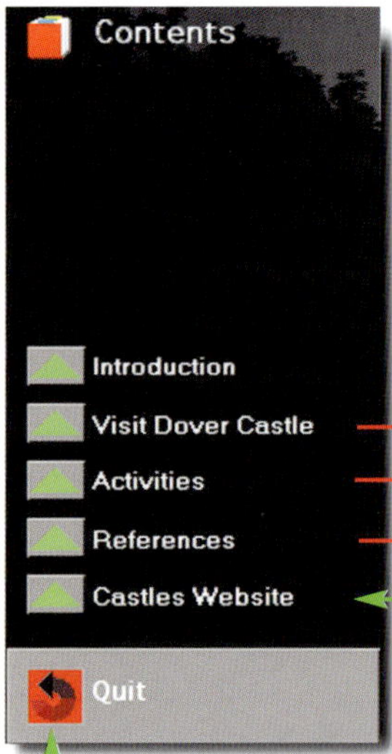

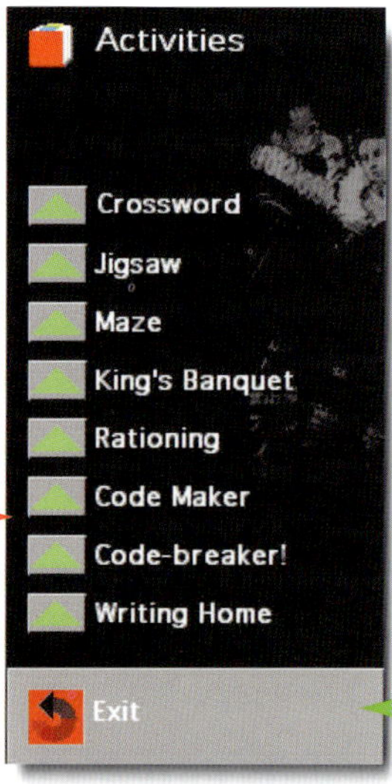

Activities

Click here to select one of the on-screen activities. (Some have optional print-out facilities.)

Click here to go back to the contents menu

Click here to quit the Real Castles CD-ROM

Click here to launch the Real Castles web site

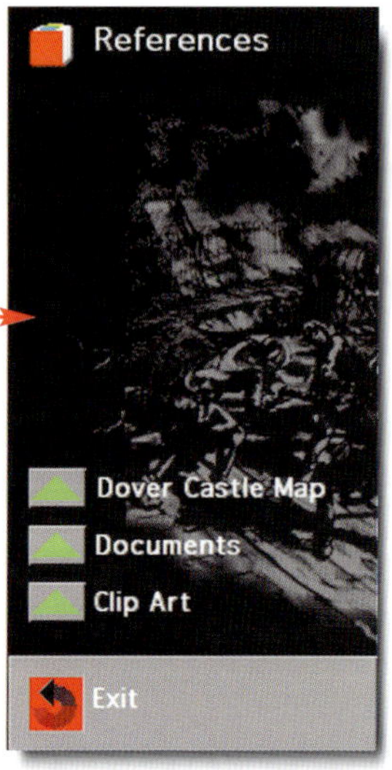

References

Click here for additional information including maps and other references.

Moving around the castle sites is easy. Just click on the arrow buttons to explore for yourself.

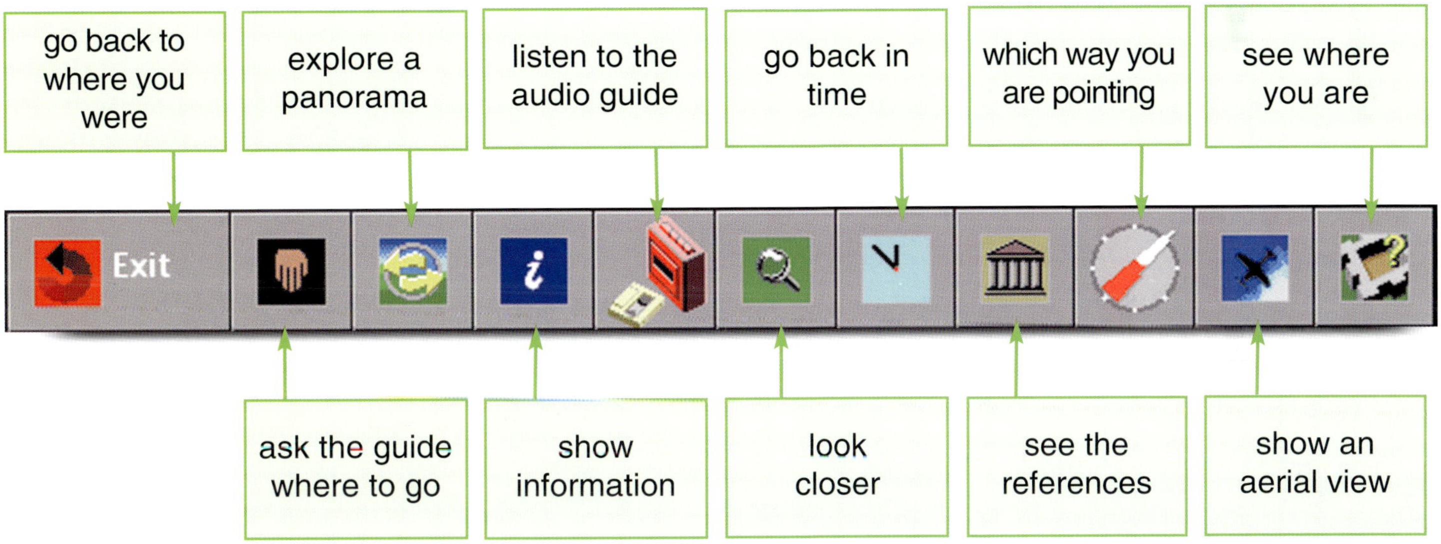

The CD also provides a library of useful clip art that you can use in your own work. This is in JPEG format and can be imported into other applications, such as MS Office or Paint on a Windows PC, ClarisWorks on a Macintosh (see page 42).

There are also a number of useful Internet links, accessed directly from the *Real Castles* web page (see page 44.) Always remember to tell an adult when you are going on-line. Of course, the best way to find out about *Real Castles* is to sit back and explore…

What is a castle?

The name castle has been given to many places which have been fortified with walls, banks of earth and ditches.

Towns in prehistoric and Roman times (see page 22) were sometimes fortified. But we usually use the word castle for a special type of medieval building.

A medieval castle was built to protect one person, the lord, and to be his family home. It was also the place where he conducted the business concerning his lands. The lands were given to him by the king in exchange for military support in times of war. The lord's lands provided him with wealth from his crops and animals.

Knights and squires

There were different types of knights. Household knights lived in the castle and attended on their lord. Other knights guarded the castle and the lands. Squires were young trainee knights. As well as learning how to ride and fight, squires looked after the horses and served at table.

MAKE YOUR OWN GATEHOUSE

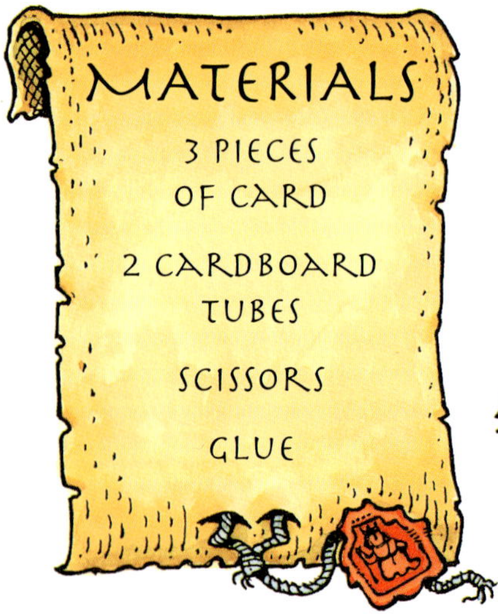

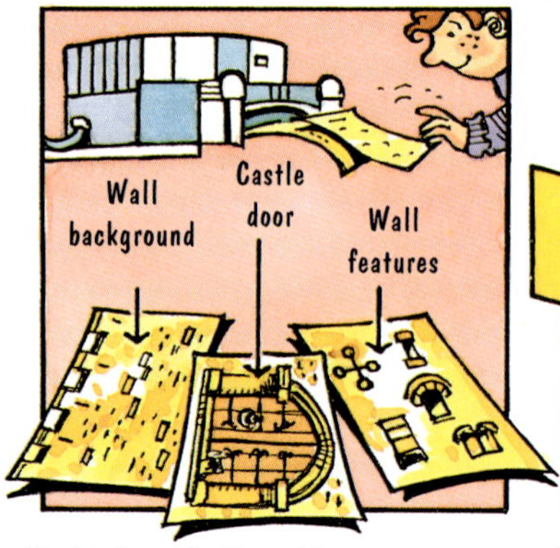

Print off the three sheets from Clip Art on the CD-ROM.

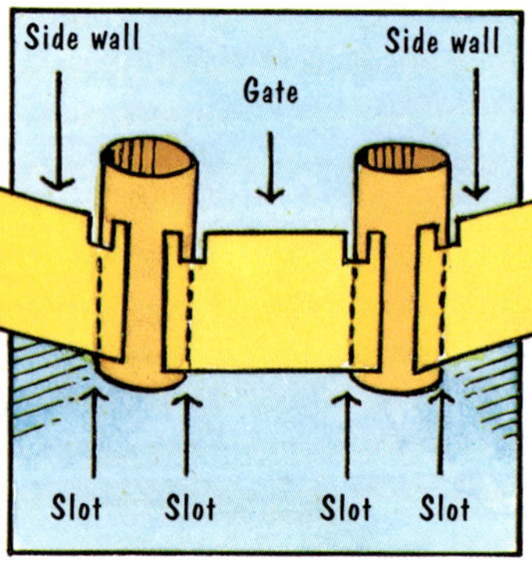

Cut slots in the tubes and card so that they link together.

Now paste on the wall sheets, door and arrow slits.

Who's who?

Many different people had special jobs to do in the castle. Among them were:

THE CHAMBERLAIN
LOOKED AFTER THE LORD'S CHAMBER AND EMPLOYED OTHERS TO TAKE CARE OF THE CHESTS OF MONEY AND OTHER GOODS.

THE CHAPLAIN
WAS THE LORD'S PRIEST AND, APART FROM CONDUCTING SERVICES IN THE CASTLE CHAPEL, KEPT THE LORD'S OFFICIAL SEAL FOR DOCUMENTS.

THE STEWARD
(USUALLY A KNIGHT) WAS IN CHARGE OF RUNNING THE CASTLE AND WAS THE MOST IMPORTANT OFFICIAL. HE SUPERVISED THE LORD'S COURT AND LOOKED CAREFULLY AT THE CASTLE'S EXPENSES.

THE KEEPER OF THE WARDROBE
WAS IN CHARGE OF THE LORD'S CLOTHES. TAILORS AND LAUNDRESSES WORKED FOR HIM.

THE MARSHAL
HAD A LARGE STAFF OF GROOMS (FOR THE HORSES), SMITHS (TO MAKE AND MEND IRON GOODS), CLERKS (TO KEEP THE ACCOUNTS) AND CARTERS (TO CARRY GOODS TO AND FROM THE CASTLE).

- **Investigate the three gates at Dover Castle.**
- **Complete the castle crossword puzzle.**

Defending the land

From prehistoric to modern times, kings and military commanders have built a variety of defences to protect and rule their lands.

ADDED PROTECTION

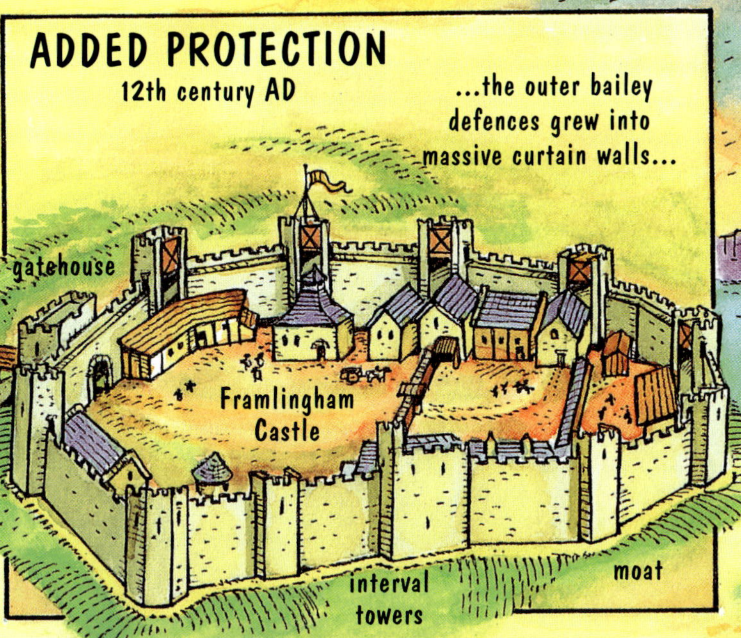

THE BEST CASTLES

HENRY VIII'S FORTS

ENGINEERS AND FORTS

MODERN WARFARE

- Explore the different periods of Dover's history.
- Find the Clip Art to make your own timeline of weapons and armour.

Building a castle

A castle might take over ten years to construct and cost millions of pounds in today's money.

Hundreds, even thousands, of skilled workers and labourers were needed for the job.

MAKE YOUR OWN ARROW SLIT

MATERIALS
- TAPE-MEASURE
- PAPER OR CARD
- COLOUR PENCILS
- SCISSORS
- BLU TACK/TAPE

Measure and cut paper to fit your bedroom window.

Draw onto it, colour and cut out a 'cruciform' arrow slit.

Stick it onto the window and prepare to defend the house!

- Find out how Dover Castle was altered after the siege of 1216.
- Find examples of other types of arrow slits.

Attack!

To starve a castle into surrender took a long time so...

❂ **Find the trebuchet and see how it fired.**

❂ **Choose the easiest part of Dover Castle to attack.**

Defence!

All castles were different but all used many ways to defend themselves...

The site of the castle was important, a hill or a river made it defendable.

- Choose the most difficult part of Dover Castle to defend.
- Find out how attackers could be trapped in the medieval tunnels.

Sleeping and eating

A castle was not just a place to be besieged in - it was also a home.

Sometimes the number of the lord's family and servants swelled into hundreds if the king visited.

The Great Hall at Warkworth Castle.

The Hall at Conisborough Castle.

The great hall

This was where everyone ate and where the lord held court and welcomed guests. It was often the best room in the castle and usually had a high ceiling, very large windows, and pictures painted on the plastered walls.

MAKE YOUR OWN HONEY TOASTS

Taking care, simmer the honey and spices for 2 minutes.

Make some toast and pour the mixture over it.

Decorate with pine nuts... and eat while hot.

The kitchen

The kitchen had a large fireplace where food was boiled in cauldrons or roasted on spits. In the walls were large dome-shaped ovens, and there was a stone trough for washing or preparing food. Drains leading to the outside wall carried away the rubbish. Because of the danger of fire, the kitchen was sometimes a separate building and was not joined to the hall.

A reconstruction of a bedroom at Dover Castle as it might have been at the time of Henry VIII's visit in 1539.

Bedrooms

The lord of the castle and his family had their own rooms in the castle keep. Everyone else slept where they could, often curled up on the floor of the great hall.

- Visit the royal apartments in the keep.
- Print out some medieval recipes and try them out.

Pastimes and sport

The favourite pastime for most lords was hunting animals, on horseback or on foot, or using birds of prey.

Some castles, such as Pickering Castle in North Yorkshire, were especially popular with kings because of the hunting nearby. Whole forests were set aside for hunting, although they were also well managed and provided a valuable building material - timber.

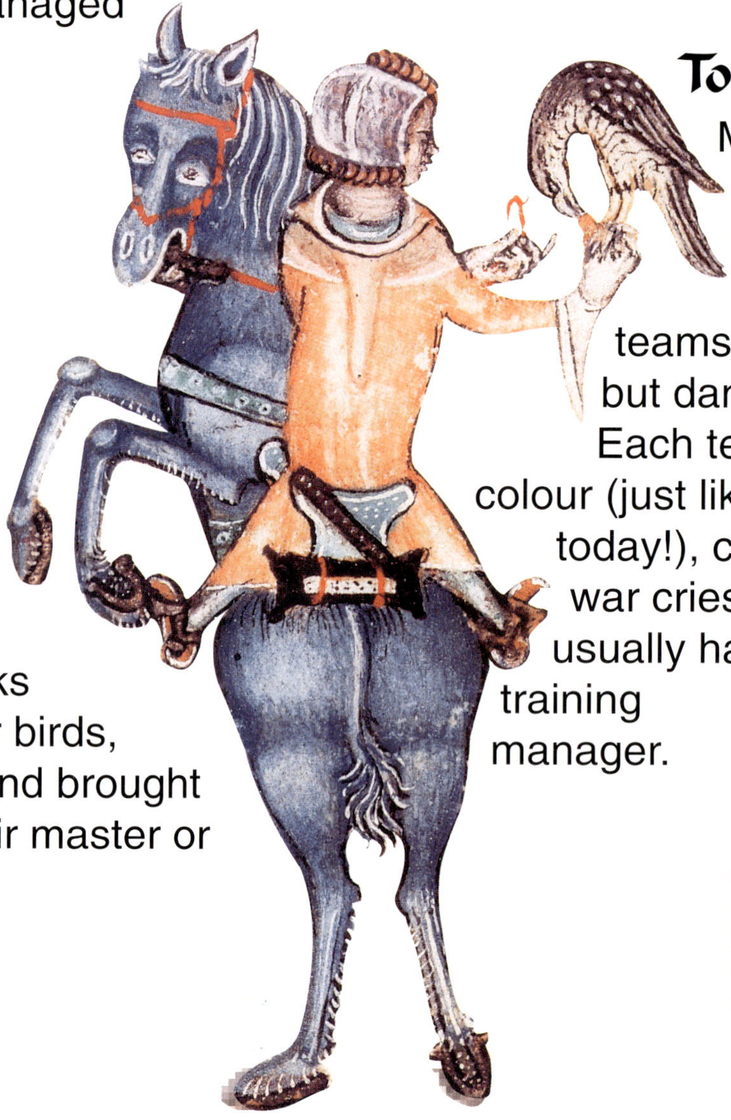

Falconry

A popular form of hunting was to use birds of prey which were especially trained to hunt small animals. Falcons and hawks went after smaller birds, rabbits or hares and brought them back for their master or mistress.

Tournaments

Medieval people enjoyed watching war games. Knights formed teams to clash in mock, but dangerous, battles. Each team wore its own colour (just like football teams today!), chanted special war cries, and usually had a training manager.

- Find the rules to play Fox and Geese.
- Can you get out of the medieval maze?

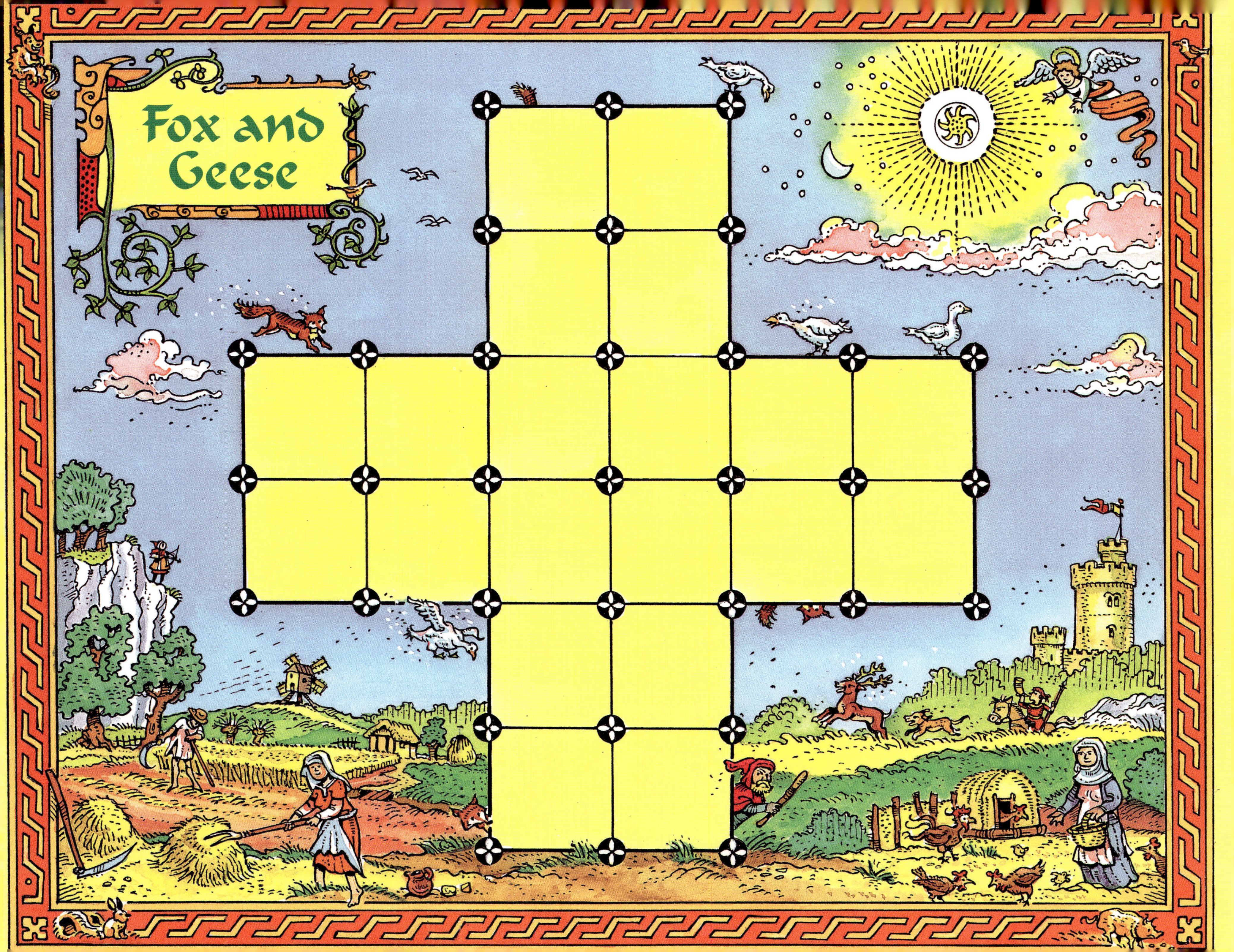
Fox and Geese

Iron Age hillforts had massive earth defences.

Defending an Iron Age hillfort against Roman attack.

Ancient Forts

In prehistoric times the first fortified places in Britain were constructed out of earth and wood, and in some cases of stone.

The prehistoric fortified places we call hillforts today were actually small towns. They had massive earth banks and ditches around the outside to keep people safe. When the Romans came to Britain they drove the people out of these hillforts and settled them in specially-built towns.

CELTS PAINTED THEMSELVES WITH WARLIKE DESIGNS USING A PLANT CALLED WOAD.

Re-enacting Celtic warfare.

Inside a hillfort were houses barns and workshops.

Hadrian's Wall, northern Britain.

Building Hadrian's Wall.

But the Romans also conquered and controlled their new territory by building forts for their army units. In one place in northern Britain the Romans even built a huge wall to protect the frontier - a defence called Hadrian's Wall.

After the Roman period, in Anglo-Saxon times, some peoples constructed earthworks to protect their own territory. The best known of these earthworks is Offa's Dyke, built by the Anglo-Saxon King Offa around AD 800. The Anglo-Saxons also built fortified towns called burghs (see page 25).

OFFA'S DYKE MAY HAVE BEEN BUILT TO STOP CATTLE RUSTLING.

The fortified Iron Age hill fort at Old Sarum, Wiltshire.

Reconstructed Roman cavalry fort, at the Lunt near Coventry.

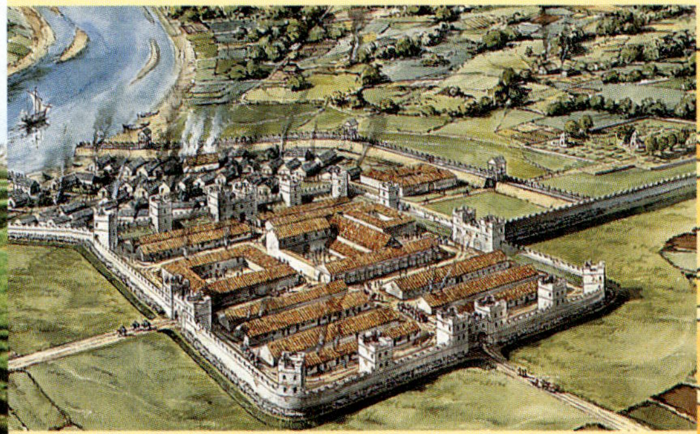

Wallsend Roman fort, Hadrian's Wall.

FOCUS ON... Dover - before the castle

People in the distant past used the top of the chalk cliffs that now look out over the town of Dover and across the Channel to France to build defences for themselves.

Over a thousand years before the first castle at Dover, prehistoric people built a defended settlement here - usually called a hillfort. This was the period we call the Iron Age, just before the Romans arrived. They dug out deep ditches and piled the earth up to make massive banks which enclosed a large area. On top of the banks they built timber walls to keep their enemies out. To get past the entrance, the enemy had to pass between steep banks and through strong wooden gates. While they tried to break the gates down, those inside could hurl down missiles!

They could keep their animals safe inside the enclosure and they built circular houses for themselves here.

MAKE YOUR OWN HILLFORT GATEWAY

Dampen the compost and dig a ditch and bank.

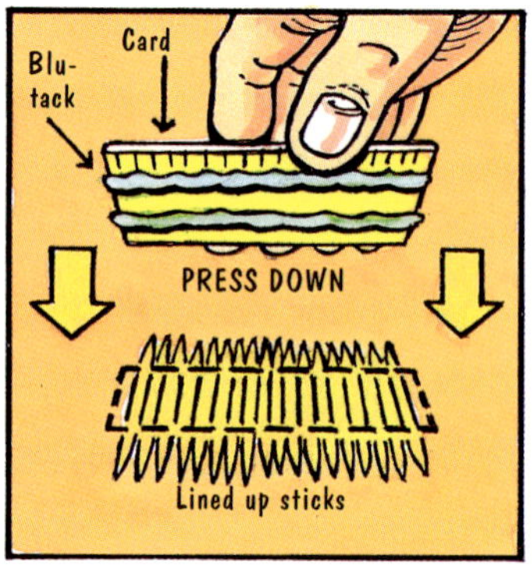

Make a palisade in sections.

Slot in the palisade and add other features.

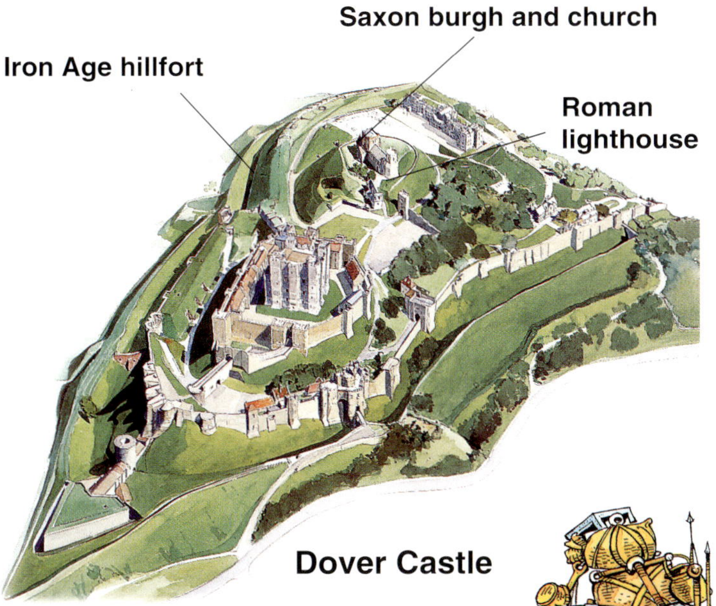

Dover Castle

The lighthouse and church at Dover Castle.

The Romans arrive!

When the Romans arrived in Britain (AD 43), they built a town and a port in the valley below. The hillfort was abandoned but the Romans found a good use for this hilltop. They built a lighthouse here (and one on the opposite hill) to guide ships into the busy port.

After the Romans

The lighthouse went out of use after the Roman period, but around AD 1000 an Anglo-Saxon church was built right next to it (reusing some of its stone and tile). The church was probably the centre of a fortified town inside the prehistoric enclosure. The Anglo-Saxons called towns like these burghs. In the 15th century the top of the Roman lighthouse was rebuilt as a bell-tower for the church.

The Roman lighthouse at Dover Castle is well preserved - in fact it is the only one in Britain. It originally had eight stages, tapering towards the top which was 24 metres above ground. At the top a fire in a metal cage shone out across the sea.

- **Find out where the best view of the lighthouse is.**
- **Find the entrance to Dover's hillfort.**

Medieval Castles

Medieval castles come in many shapes and sizes and you can expect to find the remains of one in the area you live in.

When the Normans invaded Britain in AD 1066, they brought with them the idea of the castle. The simplest fortification was called a ringwork - a bank and ditch with wooden buildings inside to protect the military garrison.

THE NORMANS EVEN BROUGHT HORSES WITH THEM.

The great motte and Clifford's Tower, York.

Building the great gate at York in the 13th century.

The castle at Richmond, North Yorkshire, dominates the town.

The great Norman keep and earthworks at Orford Castle.

Harlech Castle in Wales in the early 14th century.

The first real castle was the motte and bailey. The motte was a very large mound of earth formed by digging the earth out of a deep ditch around its base. The motte often had a timber tower on its top and was the last place to be defended if the castle was attacked. The bailey was full of buildings for the lord, his family, servants and nights.

Gradually timber and earth castles were improved in stone. The tower on the motte was replaced in stone or a stone keep was built as the most fortified part of the castle.

HUNDREDS OF SAXON HOUSES WERE DESTROYED TO MAKE ROOM FOR NORMAN CASTLES.

Kenilworth Castle in the Norman period.

The keep and towers of Goodrich Castle.

Old Sarum in about 1090.

Middleham Castle in the 14th century.

The 14th-century castle at Nunney, Somerset.

FOCUS ON... Dover - the medieval castle

During the medieval period Dover Castle was added to several times until it became one of the strongest and most up-to-date castles in Europe.

William the Conqueror's soldiers building a motte and bailey castle at Hastings. The one at Dover would have looked the same (see page 10).

The first castle

We know that there has been a castle in Dover since November 1066. It was William the Conqueror who came here after the famous Battle of Hastings and constructed a castle from earth and wood.The illustrated story of the battle can still be seen on the Bayeux Tapestry.

A castle made of stone

In 1180, King Henry II instructed his architect, called Maurice the Engineer, to build him a new castle at Dover. This time it was to be of stone. Henry II wanted the castle to

MAKE YOUR OWN SHIELD

Draw, then cut out, a shield shape and two strips of card.

Glue the strips to pull the shield into a curved shape.

Now add the design and colour - then stride forth!

be a place to live as well as a powerful fortress to defend the country. Maurice constructed a keep over 25 metres high surrounded by a courtyard, which was protected by a strong, high wall with guard towers.

Dover Castle as it was in the 13th century.

More and more defences

By the 13th century additional defences had been constructed to make Dover Castle even more difficult to break into. Outer walls were built with guard towers and heavily-defended gateways.

Siege!

During the reign of King John, Dover Castle suffered a most dramatic siege. A French army, commanded by Prince Louis, the son of the King of France, sailed to Dover to claim the English throne. Louis' troops hurled stones against the walls and dug a mine under the main gate and collapsed one of the towers. French knights and soldiers poured into the castle but the constable, Hubert de Burgh, and his knights drove them out.

The siege of Dover Castle in 1216.

❂ Find out about the siege of Dover in 1216.

❂ Print out the plan of Dover Castle and mark on the 13th-century defences.

Deal Castle in Tudor times.

One of Henry VIII's coastal castles at Deal.

Tudor Castles

In later medieval times castles began to be more like homes than places to be defended against attack from an enemy. In Tudor times forts, not castles, defended England from invasion.

The buildings in the castle's bailey were often knocked down and rebuilt. Instead of storage areas and stables for the horses of knights, the lord might build a splendid hall for himself and his family.

FOUR-POSTERS WERE IDEAL FOR DRAUGHTY HOMES.

Kenilworth Castle at the time of Queen Elizabeth's visit.

Queen Elizabeth I visits Kenilworth Castle.

One of the main living rooms at Warkworth Castle.

Besieging Old Wardour Castle during the English Civil War.

New kitchens of stone were built, along with private rooms for the family and perhaps a new chapel. The keep was used much more for storage or as a place for the less important officials. In 1538 England faced the threat of a massive invasion from Europe. The Tudor king, Henry VIII, decided to build a whole series of fortifications along the south coast of England. But these were not really castles. They were lived in, but only by small numbers of soldiers. They were forts where long-range cannons could fire on enemy ships if they sailed up the English Channel.

TUDOR FASHION TIP: BLACK OUT YOUR FRONT TEETH TO DISGUISE THE ROTTEN ONES.

Henry VIII's fort at Pendennis.

Pendennis Castle was later modernised by Elizabeth I.

Re-enacting a battle from the English Civil War.

FOCUS ON... Dover – the great keep

The great keep of Dover Castle was one of the largest and strongest in the whole country. Some of its walls are over 6 metres thick!

War

In wartime or under siege the keep was a place to store food and weapons. Soldiers stood guard at the staircases and on the roof. To get into the keep attackers needed to fight their way up the stairs in the building which protected the entrance. Apart from several sets of heavy wooden doors to break through, there was a portcullis half way up! People had to use the spiral staircases to reach the upper floors. Look at the CD-ROM to see how they worked.

Peace

In peacetime it was a place for the king and his court to live in, when they visited. Look at the picture of the keep opposite and see how the various rooms were used. Halls were used for eating, receiving guests and holding court. Bedrooms and garderobes (lavatories) were built into the thick walls.

MAKE YOUR OWN CHAIN MAIL

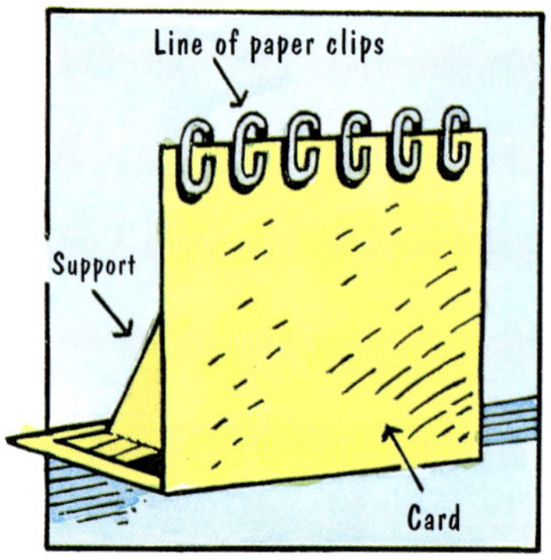

Make a display board with the paper clips on top.

Now fit a garden tie to each clip.

Next fit a tie onto each pair of ties - create an exhibit.

Henry VIII arrives!

Medieval kings and queens travelled with enormous numbers of people (their court) from castle to castle. They often ate the owners out of house and home, literally! King Henry VIII came to his own Dover Castle in March 1539 and his court had about 800 people in it. As usual for a royal visit, the castle keep was repaired and workers and craftspeople were sent ahead to install apartments fit for a king.

Reconstruction of a throne used by Henry VIII on his visit.

Dover Castle keep.

Second floor - the king's apartments

Roof - there were heavy guns here in the 18th century

Dover Castle keep had a grand, fortified entrance of staircases which brought visitors to the king's apartments on the second floor

First floor - rooms for less important members of the royal household

Basement - mainly used for storage

Entrance

❂ Find out who was who in Henry VIII's court.

❂ Take a tour of the keep.

Modern Forts

Tilbury Fort was built to withstand fire from all directions.

Martello towers were built to resist invasion by Napoleon.

Re-enacting fighting in Victorian times.

Medieval castles were often rebuilt to make sure that cannons and artillery weapons could be used on their walls. Modern military installations are different.

WHEN IS A WORM NOT A WORM? WHEN IT'S USED TO CLEAN OUT A GUN.

Enemies from across the Channel threatened to invade Britain in the 17th and 18th centuries. Tudor fortifications were rebuilt or added to. Huge triangular gun platforms were protected by walls and earth banks.

Fort Brockhurst, one of the new type of 19th-century forts.

Tudor Hurst Castle was refortified in the 19th and 20th centuries.

Preparing to fire at Pendennis Castle in about 1860.

By the 19th century warfare had changed. Huge artillery guns were hidden inside some of the old forts but there was a greater need for a completely different sort of defence.

Guns to combat the threat of attack from the air were also put inside forts, and even on castles. But there was still the threat of invasion. In the Second World War new types of fortification were built in Britain - from airfields and anti-tank defences to small, heavily fortified positions called pillboxes.

IN 1803 NAPOLEON HAD TWO THOUSAND SHIPS BUILT FOR HIS INVADING FORCE OF 100,000 TROOPS.

A pillbox on the east coast of Britain.

A factory making shells during the First World War.

Second World War observation post at Pendennis Castle.

A fort built in the Thames during the Second World War.

Bomb damage in Dover during the Second World War.

FOCUS ON... Dover - secret wartime tunnels

Long after Dover had been England's most important medieval castle, it became a secret underground headquarters for warfare in the 20th century.

Underground barracks in the 18th century.

Dover Castle had many alterations over the centuries. Henry VIII had platforms built for huge guns to protect the harbour below. Much later, in the 18th century, gun batteries were added and the threat of invasion from France meant that more fortifications, as well as barracks for soldiers, were built. It was at this time that tunnels were excavated in the chalk cliffs to provide underground barracks. Over 2000 soldiers lived below ground and had to sleep two in a bed.

MAKE YOUR OWN SECRET NOTEBOOK

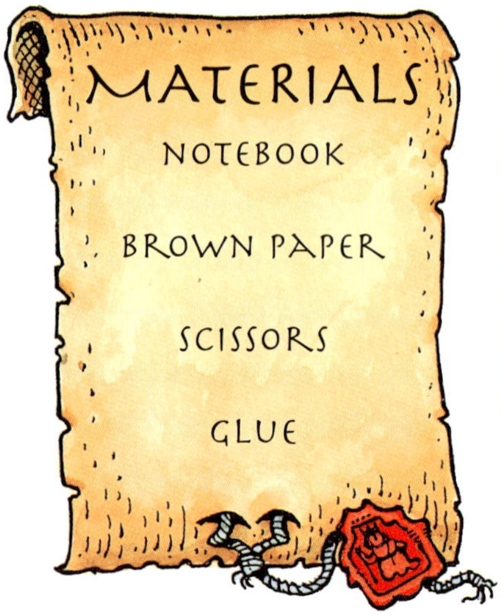

Print the 'Secret labels' sheet from the CD-ROM.

Cover the notebook and choose your secret labels.

Stick these on the cover and begin your secret operations!

World wars

In the First World War, the tunnels were used mainly to store ammunition. Some of the soldiers heading across the Channel for battle may also have stayed here before embarking from the harbour. But it was in the Second World War that this underground complex found a completely new use. At the outbreak of war in 1939 the 18th-century tunnels were turned into bomb-proof military headquarters.

Life underground

The tunnels were transformed and added to. They now formed separate, hidden and secure centres of operations for the Army, the Air Force and the Navy. Kitchens were added, a telephone communications centre constructed, and there was even a hospital for wounded soldiers returning from battles in Europe. It was from here that Vice-Admiral Bertram Ramsay directed the evacuation of Allied troops from Dunkirk in France in May 1940.

Reconstructed telephone exchange from 1941.

Modern times

Even after the Second World War, the underground tunnels were re-fitted in the 1960s to become a secret government operations centre in case of a nuclear war.

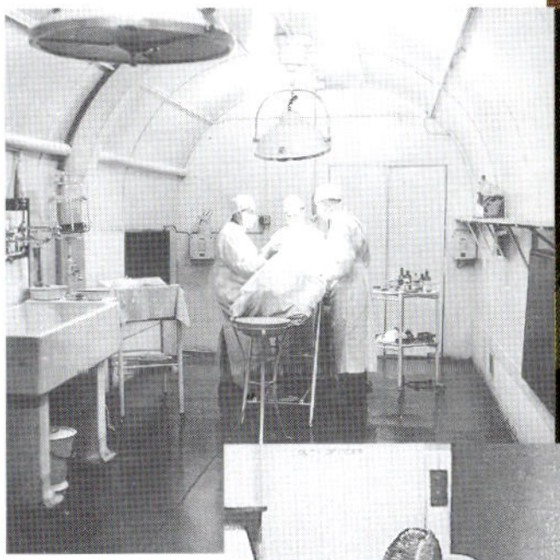

❂ Are you a good Code Breaker or an even better Code Maker?

❂ Find the plan of the secret wartime tunnels.

Document detective

Pictures and documents are good sources of evidence, if you are investigating castle ruins. Look out for them in castle guidebooks or reference books in your local library.

Pictures

Medieval manuscripts often had colour illustrations. They give us a good idea of what people wore and what they looked like.

A lady and her maid from a 14th-century manuscript. Except for those attending a lady, there were very few women servants in a castle.

Documents

Anything written at the time medieval castles were used is good evidence for a castle detective. Sometimes you will find the language rather difficult - don't despair! Look up words you don't know in a dictionary.

Interesting but true?

Can we believe everything we read? People will often give their own point of view in what they write. Here are parts of two medieval accounts, written by different people, of the same event - the siege of Dover Castle by the French in 1216.

MAKE YOUR OWN SCROLL

Print an illuminated letter from the CD-ROM and colour it.

Tape the ends onto the paper and add an impressive seal.

Now give yourself the title you deserve!

The siege through English eyes

Louis, with a powerful force of knights and soldiers laid siege to Dover Castle having sent for a mangonel from France. The French disposed this and other engines before the castle and began to batter the walls incessantly. But Hubert de Burgh, a brave knight, with a hundred and forty knights and a large number of soldiers who were defending the castle, destroyed many of the enemy, until the French feeling their loss removed their tents and engines further from the castle. At this Louis was greatly enraged and swore he would not leave the place till the castle was taken and all the garrison hung. Therefore, to strike terror into the English, the French built a number of shops and other buildings in front of the entrance to the castle......for they hoped that by hunger and protracted siege they would force them to surrender as they could not subdue them by force of arms.

Written by an English monk in the 13th century.

The siege through French eyes

That day, the English King came to Sandwich, and saw Louis' fleet. Then King John was much disheartened. He rode for a while on the shore and had his trumpets sounded, but did not give much joy to his forces, and did not encourage them much and made a very poor appearance. When he had been there a while, he left them furtively, and went very fast to Dover. Next day, he went away, leaving Hubert de Burgh, who was Justiciar of England, at Dover to guard the castle and many other knights. A very strong garrison remained in the castle. There were at least a hundred and forty knights and a great number of men at arms, and there was plenty of food.

From a 13th-century French manuscript.

- **Read about the siege of Rochester Castle.**
- **Use Clip Art to make your own medieval-style document.**

Castle detective

A police detective looks for clues to solve a crime. If you follow the trail of evidence in a ruined castle, you will soon be able to work out the castle clues and come up with a good story, or hi-story!

Be prepared

Before you visit a ruined castle, you need to make preparations.

MAKE YOUR OWN STAINED GLASS

Draw a simple design and cover with polythene.

Cut out the shapes in tissue and stick on to the polythene.

When dry, peel off the tissue, trim the edges... and admire!

....clues about defence

Murder holes to fire directly down on the enemy.

Slit for the portcullis to be lifted up.

Holes cut into the wall behind a door to hold a timber beam to stop the door being battered down.

Arrow slits in walls.

.....clues about building construction

Putlog holes for wooden beams show where there was once a floor.

Fireplaces high up on a wall show there are now floors missing.

.....clues about living in a castle

Remains of garderobe (lavatory) ....and the shoot where the (ugh!) flowed out through the castle's walls.

Drains in walls show where washing was done.

- Make your own 'I-spy Castle Clues' checklist.
- Which is your favourite part of Dover Castle?

Real Castles clip art

These images are all stored in a folder called 'Clip Art' on the *Real Castles* CD.

You can import or insert the clip art directly into your word processor from the 'File' menu. Alternatively, if you have an application that loads JPEG files directly, such as Internet Explorer, simply double-click on a clip art file.

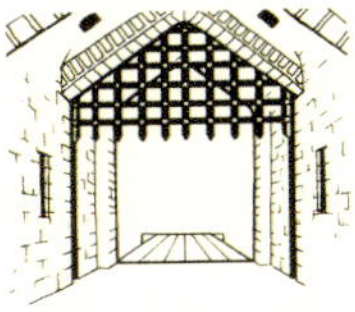

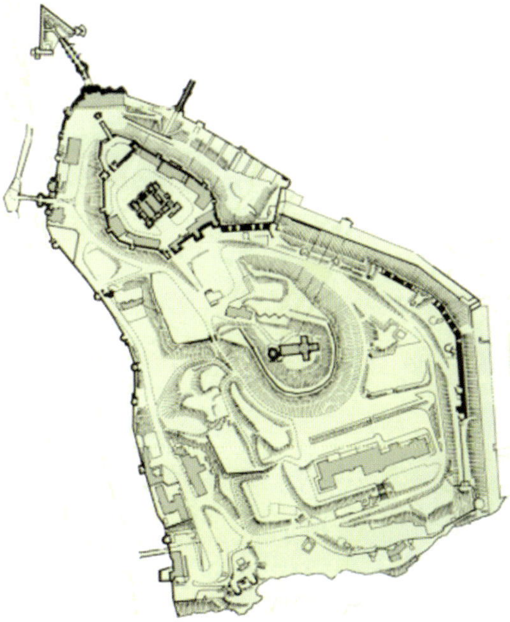

What other pieces of clip art can you find in the clip art folder?

Real Castles on the web

If you have an Internet connection you can find out lots more about castles on-line. This section contains a selection of useful links to important castle web sites.

You will need

- a modem connected to your PC
- a Web Browser (such as Netscape Navigator, or Microsoft Explorer)
- an Internet service connection (such as Demon or AOL)

- Launch your browser and connect up to the Internet
- Type in: http://www.tagdev.co.uk/realcastles.htm
- Choose from the list of links and find out lots more about castles

School sites

Virtual tour of Skipton Castle
Burley Middle School
Virtual tour of Skipton castle with pictures and information created by pupils

School visit to Richmond
Burnhope Primary School
Pictures from a visit to Richmond castle in N. Yorkshire

History links for children
Highdown School
Links to medieval history resources

Sites for children

The Tower of London
Camelot International
Pictures, information, maps and QTVR panoramic views

Castle Explorer
National Geographic
Interactive tour of a virtual castle

Glossary of Castle Terms
Castles on the Web
Comprehensive glossary of castle terms

Motte and Bailey Castles
Jeffrey L. Thomas
Information and pictures explaining motte and bailey castles

Siegecraft and Defence
Jeffrey L. Thomas
Information and pictures explaining siege engines

Free Castle Pictures
FreeFoto
Collection of free photographs including many castles from across the UK

Medieval Cookery
Gode Cookery
Pictures, information and medieval recipes to try out

Young Archaeologists club
Council for British Archaeology
Information about the club

Museum sites

24 Hour Museum
24 Hour Museum home page
Information about the museum's virtual galleries

British Museum
British Museum home page
Information about the museum's galleries, exhibitions and events

Imperial War Museum
Imperial Museum home page
Information about the museum's galleries, exhibitions and events

Sites for teachers and parents

Historic Snapshots
Public Records Office
Activities based on visual sources from the National Archive

The Historical Association
The Historical Association home page
Resources, articles and links about teaching history

History Channel
History Channel home page
American site dedicated to history with useful resources and links

Historic Scotland
Historic Scotland home page
Information and links from the Scottish agency for safeguarding Scotland's built heritage

Monuments in Northern Ireland
Northern Ireland environment and heritage service
Information and links from the Northern Ireland environment and heritage service

CADW Welsh Historic Monuments
CastleWales
Information on joining CADW Welsh historic monuments

English Heritage
English Heritage home page
Pictures, links and information for sites across the country

TAG Developments Ltd
TAG's home page
Information about other software, resources and training

Link sites

Castles on the Web
Castles on the Web home page
Links, photographs and information about castles from around the world

National Museums of Scotland
National Museums of Scotland home page
Information and links to many Scottish museums and collections online

Castle Wales
Jeffrey L. Thomas
Information, links and photographs on over 400 Welsh castles

Historic Irish Castles
Jim Moats
Pictures, information and Quicktime video clips from a selection of Irish castles

UK Museums
MuseumNet home page
Comprehensive listing of links to museums across the UK

BBC History Web Guide
BBC Online
Regularly updated selection of history web sites

The Ancient World
Web links
If you can't find what you're looking for at any of these sites, you could make your own search:
1. Launch your browser and connect up to the Internet
2. Type in: http://www.yahoo.com
3. Type in some words to make your search

castle
medieval
siege
knights
heraldry

Glossary

BAILEY courtyard area, enclosed by an outer wall, full of buildings for living in, storage and animals

BARBICAN outer defence of a castle's main gate

BARRACKS soldiers' living quarters

BASTION tower or gun platform projecting beyond the castle walls

BAYEUX TAPESTRY the story of the Battle of Hastings embroidered in coloured wools on linen

BELFRY siege tower to allow attackers to reach the top of the outer walls

BURGH fortified place in Saxon times

CANNON large gun which used gunpowder to fire the ball, often made of stone

CONSTABLE a knight appointed to be in charge of a castle while the owner (often the king) was away

COURT a large number of people who attended on the king and went with him from place to place

DOODLEBUG name given to the V-1 German flying bombs which began dropping on London in June 1944

DRAWBRIDGE a removable bridge into a castle

ENGLISH CIVIL WAR fought from 1642 to 1651 between the supporters of the king (Cavaliers) and Parliament (Roundheads)

GARDEROBE lavatory, usually built into the castle walls

GATEHOUSE tower built over a gate to defend it

GARRISON group of soldiers who were based in a castle or a fort

HILLFORT defended hilltop town in pre-Roman times

KEEP large, heavily fortified tower used to live in

MANGONEL catapult for hurling stones

MANUSCRIPT hand-written document

MANTLET large but moveable wooden shield

MARTELLO TOWER small brick fort to guard the coast of England against invasion from Napoleon

MOAT deep ditch (often filled with water) around a castle for extra defence

MORTAR mixture of lime and sand used to hold stone together in building walls

MOTTE large mound of earth to support a wooden tower

MURDER HOLES openings in ceilings to allow missiles to be dropped on an enemy

PILLBOX small gun position to attack an invasion force

PORTCULLIS door lowered to shut off a castle's entrance

PUTLOG HOLES holes left in walls to take the timbers to support a floor or scaffolding for repair

SALLY-PORT small door (port) in an outer wall to allow those inside to 'sally' out to attack a besieging army

SIEGE to surround and attack a castle or town to try to force those inside to surrender

SQUIRE an apprentice knight serving as a personal servant

TOURNAMENT a practice fight for a group of knights

TREBUCHET a large catapult for hurling stones, and other missiles

Find the crossword on the CD-ROM for more useful words.

Useful addresses

English Heritage
23 Savile Row
London W1X 1AB

TAG Developments Ltd
25 Pelham Road
Gravesend
Kent DA11 OHU

Young Archaeologists Club
Bowes Morrell House
111 Walmgate
York YO1 9WA

Dover Castle Kent,
on the east side of Dover town, is the English Heritage castle featured in this book/CD-ROM.

Other castles to visit

There are hundreds of castles and forts to visit in Britain. Many are ruined but can still be explored. A few are very well preserved with reconstructed rooms and exhibitions. You will find others if you connect to the special web sites for this book (see page 44). The largest museums in the country will have collections of objects from the medieval period, but try your local museum first. Here is a list of the other medieval and later castles and forts mentioned or illustrated in this book:

Clifford's Tower, York. One of the two medieval castles in York survives as a stone tower on a huge motte of earth.

Conisborough Castle, South Yorkshire. Huge and magnificent 12th-century keep.

Deal Castle, Kent. Built by Henry VIII as an artillery fortress which once carried 66 guns.

Fort Brockhurst, Hampshire. A 19th-century artillery fort built to protect Portsmouth harbour.

Goodrich Castle, Hereford & Worcester. Almost complete castle to explore with remains from the 12th to the 14th centuries.

Harlech Castle, Gwynedd, Wales. Built by Edward I between 1283 and 1289 on a cliff-top.

Hurst Castle, Hampshire. Originally a Henry VIII fortress which was strengthened in the 19th and 20th centuries.

Kenilworth Castle, Warwickshire. A Norman castle but greatly altered over time, in particular for the visits of Queen Elizabeth I.

Middleham Castle, North Yorkshire. The castle, built in the 12th century, was the childhood home of King Richard III.

Nunney Castle, Somerset. A small 14th-century moated castle.

Old Sarum, Wiltshire. This prehistoric hillfort was reused as the outer defences of the Norman castle.

Old Wardour Castle, Wiltshire. Built in the late 14th century but badly damaged in the Civil War.

Orford Castle, Suffolk. Tall and well-preserved keep built by Henry II.

Pendennis Castle, Cornwall. One of a chain of castle forts built by Henry VIII but re-fortified and used through to the Second World War.

Pickering Castle, North Yorkshire. A large motte with a shell keep built on top.

Richmond Castle, North Yorkshire. A large castle built by William the Conqueror.

Tilbury Fort, Essex. Best preserved example of 17th-century artillery fort in England, built to defend the Thames and the route into London.

Warkworth Castle, Northumberland. Massive 14th-century keep survives as an example of a fortified residence.